1❤1
VALENTINE JOKES

by Pat Brigandi
Illustrated by Don Orehek

SCHOLASTIC INC.
New York Toronto London Auckland Sydney

To my funny valentines:
Joseph, Michael, Matthew,
Marissa, and Andrea

ISBN 0-590-47141-4

12 11 10 9 8 7 6 5 4 3 2 1   4 5 6 7 8 9/9

Printed in the U.S.A.   01

First Scholastic printing, January 1994

Knock, knock
Who's there?
Art.
Art who?
Arts and flowers
just for you!

"My boyfriend's name should be Grape
Smasher."
   "Why?"
   "He's such a whiner."

"My boyfriend's name should be Big Ben."

"Why?"

"Because I don't have time for him."

"My boyfriend's name should be Geometry."

"Why?"

"He's such a square."

"My girlfriend's name should be Cannon."

"Why?"

"She thinks she's such a big shot."

"My boyfriend's name should be Onion."
　"Why?"
　"Sometimes he makes me want to cry."

Did you hear what happened when Jake and Kate tried to kiss in the fog?

They mist!

Girl: My boyfriend has been telling everybody he's going to marry the most beautiful girl in the world.
Friend: Oh, what a shame. And after all the time you two have been dating!

What happened when the vampire met a beautiful woman?

It was love at first bite!

Boyfriend: My New Year's resolution is not to lose my temper.

Girlfriend: Do you really plan on keeping that resolution?

Boyfriend: Of course!

Girlfriend: Good — then you won't yell when I tell you that I lost my engagement ring this morning.

Sweet: What did one heart say to the other heart?
Heart: Nothing — organs can't talk!

Lovey: Why did the banana go out with the prune?
Dovey: It couldn't get a date!

❤ WHEN THE BEST IS STILL NOT GOOD ENOUGH FOR YOUR FAVORITE VALENTINE — SEND THESE! ❤

I'm crazy for you . . .

... but I'm also crazy about the werewolf!

You're good-looking in a way . . .

. . . far, far away!

You have a face like a saint . . .

. . . a Saint Bernard!

You're the kind you have to look at twice . . .

. . . the first time you just don't believe it!

Mary: What's sticky, green, has eighteen legs, and is covered with long, brown hair?

John: I don't know. What?

Mary: I don't know, either. But it's crawling out of that box of valentine chocolates!

Should you ever eat chocolates on an empty stomach?

No, always on a plate.

How can you change a piece of chocolate into a vegetable?

You toss it into the air and it comes down squash.

How do you say chocolate in French?

Chocolate in French.

If corn has ears and potatoes have eyes — what do chocolates have?

Each other.

Where do you usually find chocolates?

Right where you left them.

Girl: My boyfriend does bird imitations.
Friend: I didn't know he was so
talented.
Girl: He watches me like a hawk.

Girl: Honey, this boat leaks.
Boy: Only at one end, darling. We'll just sit at the other end.

❤ HEARTWARMING KNOCK, KNOCKS ❤

Knock, knock.
Who's there?
Norma Lee.
Norma Lee who?
Norma Lee I don't go around knocking
   on doors, but I just had to meet you!

Knock, knock.
Who's there?
Dishes.
Dishes who?
Dishes your one and only sweetheart.

Knock, knock.
Who's there?
Alma.
Alma who?
Alma valentine chocolates are gone!

Knock, knock.
Who's there?
Celeste.
Celeste who?
Celeste time I'm going to ask you to be
  my valentine!

Knock, knock.
Who's there?
Darryl.
Darryl who?
Darryl always be a place in my heart
for you!

Knock, knock.
Who's there?
Ivan.
Ivan who?
Ivan to be alone!

Knock, knock.
Who's there?
Lena.
Lena who?
Lena over. I want to give you a little
  kiss!

Knock, knock.
Who's there?
Boo.
Boo who?
Don't cry. I'm sure you'll get a valentine
    this year!

Knock, knock.
Who's there?
Venice.
Venice who?
Venice your boyfriend coming over?

The lovesick girl waits as the fortune-teller gazes into her crystal ball. "Do you see a boyfriend in my future?" she asks. "Yes," says the fortune-teller. "I see some good news and some bad news. The good news is that on this very night you will meet a tall, dark, and handsome stranger."

The girl couldn't believe her good fortune. "Oh, that's so exciting!" she cries. "I'm dying to meet him!" The fortune-teller raises her eyebrow. "Yes, I know. You see, the bad news is his name is Count Dracula!"

. . . you're the first to leave — and it's
your party!

. . . all the refreshments are pink and
red to match the valentine theme!

. . . they show a movie in the middle of
the party, and the star is a big purple
dinosaur!

... the invitation says *dance party*, and everyone is dressed in pink leotards and ballet slippers!

. . . after waiting all night for the really cute guy or girl to ask you to dance, you have to say "NO!" because you have to get home before curfew!

. . . you're forced to play musical chairs all night, even at the dinner table!

❤ ROSES ARE RED,
VIOLETS ARE BLUE,
HERE ARE SOME VALENTINES
THAT JUST CAN'T BE TRUE! ❤

Dear Frankenstein,

Roses are red,
Shamrocks are green,
When I look at your face,
I just want to scream.

Love,
Your bride

Dear Lou,

Roses are red,
Violets are blue,
The jeweler made me give the ring
back,
The money was due!

> Love,
> Sue

Dear Jill,

Roses are red,
Tulips are pink,
If you don't go out with me,
You're a big fink!

> With all my affection,
> Bill

Dear Teach,

Roses are red,
Violets aren't gray,
I gave you this card,
Now give me an A.

                    With love,
                    Your favorite student

Honey: Excuse me, dear. What is the meaning of these flowers on my desk today?

Bunny: Why, it's your wedding anniversary.

Honey: Is that so? Well, do let me know when yours is so I may do the same for you.

Girlfriend: I wish you'd pay a little attention to me.

Boyfriend: I'm paying as little as I can.

"My boyfriend's name is Tornado."
  "Why?"
  "He makes my head spin."

"My girlfriend's name should be Alien."
  "Why?"
  "She's out of this world."

"My boyfriend's name should be
Puzzle."
  "Why?"
  "Sometimes I can't figure him out."

"My boyfriend's name should be Jump Rope."

"Why?"

"He makes my heart skip a beat."

"My girlfriend's name should be
Refrigerator."
   "Why?"
   "She can be cold as ice."

"My boyfriend's name should be
Question Mark."
   "Why?"
   "He's such a mystery to me."

"My girlfriend's name should be Rock."
 "Why?"
 "She has a heart of stone."

Knock, knock.
Who's there?
Jimmy.
Jimmy who?
Jimmy a little kiss on the cheek.

Knock, knock.
Who's there?
Emma.
Emma who?
Emma so happy you asked me to be
   your valentine.

Knock, knock.
Who's there?
Dozen.
Dozen who?
Dozen anyone want to be my valentine?

Knock, knock.
Who's there?
Ken.
Ken who?
Ken I give you a kiss good night?

Knock, knock.
Who's there?
Ben.
Ben who?
Ben thinking a lot about you lately.

Knock, knock.
Who's there?
Eyesore.
Eyesore who?
Eyesore am glad you called.

Knock, knock.
Who's there?
Butcher.
Butcher who?
Butcher arms around me, honey, and
hold me tight.

Knock, knock.
Who's there?
Honeydew.
Honeydew who?
Honeydew you love me?

Knock, knock.
Who's there?
Lettuce.
Lettuce who?
Lettuce get married.

Will you remember me tomorrow?
Of course I will.
Will you remember me next week?
Of course I will.
Will you remember me next month?
Of course I will.
Will you remember me next year?
Of course I will.
Knock, knock.
Who's there?
See, you forgot me already!

What did the snake give his girlfriend
on their first date?

A *good-night* hiss.

Whom do birds marry?

Their tweet *hearts.*

"Did you hear the one about the lovesick frogs?"

"No. How does it end?"

". . . and they lived *hoppily* ever after."

Why did everyone call the Cyclops a playboy?

He had an eye for the ladies.

What did the short-order cook give his girlfriend when they became engaged?

A fourteen-karat onion ring.

What did one eye say to the other eye?

Just between you and me, there's something that smells.

What did one ear say to the other ear?

Between you and me we need a haircut.

What did the bee say to the rose?

Hi, bud.

What did one tonsil say to the other tonsil?

Better get ready — the doctor is taking us out tonight.

What did one candle say to the other candle?

Let's go out together.

What did one magnet say to the other magnet?

I'm attracted to you.

What did the chewing gum say to the shoe?

I'm stuck on you.

Your favorite valentine has just given you the absolute best gift ever. Now you have to say thanks. Here are some suggestions that will help you tell your loved one exactly how you feel!

Dear _____ ,

I love your wonderful gift. I plan to:

____ pour catsup on it and feed it to my cat.

____ hide it in a drawer next to the gift you gave me last year.

When I saw how beautifully wrapped the package was, I said:

_____ "It's amazing what you can do with recycled garbage these days."

_____ "Do I really have to open this?"

It's such a thoughtful gift. It's just the thing I need to:

_____ start my collection of used bottle caps.

_____ learn to snorkle in my backyard pool.

You are my favorite person in the whole world. And this is my favorite gift. It makes me so happy to know that:

_____ maybe next year you'll take the hint and give me cash.

_____ I have better taste than you do.

_____ I can take it back to the store.

You really shouldn't have.

Love,

_____

Tom: I married a girl who was one of twins.
Jerry: How do you tell them apart?
Tom: Her brother has a beard.

Mike: I've been asked to get married hundreds of times.
Marissa: By whom?
Mike: My parents.

Why is a bride always out of luck on her wedding day?

She never marries the best man.

Who can hold up a train without being arrested?

A bridesmaid at a wedding.

Why is the letter V like a newlywed?

Because it's always in love.

Will you marry me?

I can't — I'm your other end, silly!

Stupid: Did you notice how my
  girlfriend's voice filled the hall?
Cupid: Yes, I noticed that a lot of
  people left to make room for it.

Harry: What did the mad scientist use
  to mend a broken heart?
Sally: Masking tape.

Lovey: I would like you to prove that you are capable of strong, faithful, and everlasting love.

Dovey: Well, I can bring you dozens of references from other girls.

Whom did the monster take to the valentine dance?

His ghoul*friend*.

❤ VALENTINES WITH A TWIST! ❤

Share these tongue twisters with the one you love! Try to say each one ten times.

Chocolate-covered cherries.

Ken kissed Kate but Kate kicked Ken.

Harriet happily held her hearts in her hand.

Lyle loved Lila like Lila loved Lyle.

Frank frequently found fresh flowers for Franny.

Girlfriend: Did you send my
   Valentine's Day card air mail?
Boyfriend: Yes. And I put a light on
   your mailbox to show the plane where
   to land.

Boyfriend: I had to return that alarm clock you gave me for Valentine's Day.

Girlfriend: Why?

Boyfriend: It kept going off while I was asleep.

Boyfriend: Why don't you answer the phone?

Girlfriend: It isn't ringing.

Boyfriend: Must you always wait until the last minute?

Girlfriend: How would you like a pair of bookends for Valentine's Day?

Boyfriend: That would be great. I always read the ending of a book before the beginning.

Girlfriend: Now that we're engaged, I hope you'll give me a ring.
Boyfriend: Sure, what's your number?

Cal: How do you know the math teacher, Ms. Valentine, likes you?

Sal: Likes me? She *loves* me! Look at the hugs and kisses on my math test.

Knock, knock.
Who's there?
Heart.
Heart who?
Heart you going to wish everyone a
    Happy Valentine's Day?